Late Bloomer

Late Bloomer

Prepared by TGH: The Good House Ltd.
www.TGHBooks.com

Late Bloomer

JODI VIENNEAU

DEDICATION

To my daughters, Kennedy and Kamrynn.
You never asked to be my rock in all of this, but you both
were, and are. Thank you for being you. Thank you for
looking down at me from Heaven and saying, "Her. That
is who we choose to be our mom."
It is an honour and a privilege to have a front row seat to
your amazingness. I love you both more than words could
ever express.
Love,
Mom
xoxoxoxoxoxxo

PREFACE

This will be the third time I've started writing this book. Life has a way of pressing pause when you least expect it, and usually most need it.

This is my story. Well, a portion of my story. God willing, I still have many chapters yet to come. This is the story of my coming of age. Of discovering who I am at my core. For me, this didn't happen until I was in my 40s. I've learned that life has many different "puberties" for us to go through during the course of our lives. Most coming of age tales take place in the 20s. Not me. Hence, the name of this book, "Late Bloomer".

This is not a how-to, or a fictitious tale – although some days I wonder. It's an honest sharing of what it means to go through a return to self. Some might even label this a "how NOT to", and some days, I'd agree with that too.

My purpose and hopes in sharing my growth and this journey is that in it, you will see yourself. You will then know that you are not crazy. You're not alone. You're more powerful, strong, and amazing than you even know.

Laugh with me, cry with me. Get to know me, and maybe even yourself, through the lines on each of these pages.

Jodi

"... the thought of never being kissed again
was too much
for her to bear.
The thought of living another 50 years
without passion
made her scream inside.
She was dying.
The slow, agonizing death of compromise.
She sold herself out for a version of life
that was not complete.
Not hers.
She had stuffed the very essence
of She into a dark corner and closed the
door."

Excerpt from "She Needed More"
Written by Jodi, 2015

PART ONE

1

———

Ok Jodi.
You wanted to write a book, so let's do it.
You seem to think that you have shit to share with the world.
So...starting half way through.
That's about right.
Dive right in.
Ok.
Deep breath.
Put your big girl panties on...

———

Ok so hear me out...
I've always loved writing. I love words. I love that I can control the cadence and the tone simply by placing

Words

   In different

                              Spaces.

I love that punctuation can cause the reader to stop. And then start again.
I have always dreamed of writing a book. One day I was in the shower and I heard a message from Spirit* (*my catch-all phrase for spirit guides, angels, ancestors) - did I mention that I'm a psychic and medium and this is a common occurrence — and I heard, clear as day, that I needed to write a book. I even heard the title. This title.
So, like any skeptic, I said that if this was true, then I needed to receive this message three times over the next week and then I'd believe that I was meant to do this.
Sure enough, I received the message, in various forms from "random" (human) sources over the next few days.

Divine synchronicity brought me my amazing, and patient, publisher, and here we are.

I'm neither joking nor being sarcastic when I say that I've tried to write this three times over the last 4 years. It's not as easy as one would think and the amount of discipline and focus has often been just beyond what I've been capable of.

But now it's a matter of following through. I have no idea if anyone will read it. Maybe a couple of my friends, some loyal clients, likely some haters. I promise that I will always do my best to be as honest with you as I can.

If any of you knows Oprah, send her a copy and maybe she will like it.

———

I think my story should start on November 6, 2012. My husband of 14 years had packed a bag and left during the night. I was sad, mad, exhausted, afraid…and slightly elated. We didn't have a horrible marriage. Truth be told, I'm sure we could have just stuck it out and carried on. But we both would have been miserable inside. Truly. It would have been a slow death of that spark that lives within all of us.

We met on a blind date 15 years earlier. I knew that night that I would marry him, but I also knew that he wouldn't be the love of my life. How's that for some first date insights?

We got married and had two amazing, beautiful, incredible daughters. I knew all along that I wasn't the love of his life either. I questioned if he even really loved me. But some people are meant to come together only to bring new souls into this world, and that's just how it is. And that is an incredible gift and blessing.

All of my life I had dreamed of soul-deep love. The kind that defies explanation and goes deeper than any known words. I would write poetry, songs, short stories all dedicated to this love. I would dream of it and wake up with tears streaming down my face. I feel like my soul has known this love so of course I spent my life searching for it. Remembering it.

Having an inexplicable knowledge of such a thing is both a blessing and a curse. I looked for it in everyone I dated or met. Far too often I would be drunk and delusional on the possibility of it and would give myself away to the wrong men all in the hopes that maybe this would be the one. You can therefore imagine my mixed emotions upon that first date with my soon to be husband. Knowing that I would marry him, but also knowing that he would not be the source of the love I searched for. That's not to say that I didn't love him, because I did, but I knew it wasn't *the* love.

The night that he left, I had told him that I couldn't be his roommate anymore. That the thought of living the rest of my life without being truly kissed again was making me die inside. We had a fairly decent relationship. Friends over lovers. We were financially stable. We were admired by many of our friends. But it was lacking so much. There's only so many times that the same conversation can be had with the same results before you either succumb to your fate, or you find that sliver of light and hope that is the only other option.

I think he was genuinely surprised in the moment. He's always been the steadfast one who just sucks it up and carries on. Who figures this is just the way his life is going to be and that's that, why even ever consider anything more? I'm sure that if he were to look back on it now, he would see that there's a big difference between existing and living. Between loving and cohabitating.

So, there I was. Alone in the house that we had made a home. Part of me wanted him to call and fight for us, and part of me dreaded that he would. I knew that this was God/the Universe hearing my tearful pleas. That there was more waiting for me. I remember telling my friend that the Universe had given me the opportunity of a fresh start and who was I to waste it?

Yeah, that optimism was short lived.

Not entirely, I should say. I was drunk on the thought of a second chance for me. But occasionally, that giant rejection would come barging in like the Kool-Aid man and I'd be crushed beneath that rubble. I took my marriage vows seriously. I always said that if and when I got married, it would be forever. My parents divorced. My older brother was divorced. I would be the one who went the distance. Come Hell or high water.

I know now that those are the ramblings of ego. I had no idea that in order to make it to that imagined finish line I'd have to sacrifice the very essence of who I was. Who I AM. And that was just something that I wouldn't or couldn't live with. I didn't want THAT to be the legacy of me, the legacy that I left my children.

There was so much of me that was hidden away from him, from our life. It was as though I was playing a role in a production that I didn't really sign up for. I just figured that was how it worked. I mean, all of my married friends kept parts of themselves hidden from their spouses, so that must be ok, right?

It was a strange paradox – I wanted the togetherness so badly, but as the years went by, it got increasingly harder to ignore the parts of me that were not welcome there. There were times that I felt as though I were living a double life. But, from the outside, we had it all. What a cluster fuck. Honestly. I'm exhausted just thinking about it.

But there's a certain level of security that comes with a long-term relationship, whether that relationship is fulfilling or not. There are boundaries and roles and trappings that come along with it, that create an identity. A predictability – even if it's not ideal, there's a level of comfort to be found in that.

Losing that identity, that security, and that level of comfort was something that I feared. Being judged by outsiders. Gossiped about. I had seen enough marriages end to know that the social ramifications would be big. It's funny though, you have an idea of who will stand by you and who you're sure will take the other's side, and let me tell you, you're usually wrong. So not only does it become a loss of how you define yourself in *one* aspect, but many.

So, this one step that I took towards myself, ended up being a giant step away from so many other things.

———

Good grief.
That was pretty fucking dramatic.
It reads more like a movie of the week than the beginning of
"Jodi's story".
You're doing good though.
Chapter one in the bag.
Woo hooo!
Only…wait…how many chapters is this supposed to have??
Also, this is pretty serious.
The whole thing isn't going to be like this, is it?
Well, keep going. Let's see how this all plays out…

———

It was dramatic. God knows that some days it still is. But it's real. It's the beginning of my journey to the me that would be driving the bus towards all that the rest of my life has in store. I know that many will be able to relate to all of that. To all of this. I also know that there will be many who won't be able to. That's ok. Perhaps this will be some insight and allow to you be more compassionate or empathetic when those you know are going through it.

Shall we continue?

2

There I was, 40 years old. Two beautiful daughters. A big house and a piece of land that were now my responsibility. That were haunted with the emotions and memories of the picture-perfect life that had so much going on behind the scenes.

In the years that we lived there, we had developed a routine – he did all of the outside stuff and I did the inside. I have always been fiercely independent and over time, I had lost that part of me and had become a woman that I didn't know – nor had a whole lot of respect for. The days/weeks/years that followed were filled with me getting reacquainted with my independent self. With learning and taking on the tasks that I willingly relinquished to the man of the house.

There were times when I screamed right out loud. I raged at God or the Universe or whomever was in earshot. I would be consumed with frustration at not being able to do simple things like open our sliding door to our massive steel shed. I remember being so frustrated that I couldn't slide that fucking door open. Something that I had seen my husband do a thousand times. I raged that I was not physically strong enough. I raged that he wasn't there to do it. I raged that my marriage was over. I raged that I felt like a failure in that moment. I raged that I was raging.

There were SO many times like that in the years after my marriage ended. We lived in a 4000 square foot house on 8 acres of land. That's a lot of upkeep. I had no money. I had just me and my girls. That's a boatload of DIYing. That's a lot of frustration. That's also a lot of victories. I remember the day that I took our entire dryer apart and fixed it all by myself. Or the day that my girls and I hauled truck load after truck load of stuff to the dump that my ex-husband should have done before. We celebrated so much that day. There was pride and triumph and closure in that day.

It's funny, no one really talks about all of those sorts of things that you have to face and learn when a marriage ends. There's much talk of the emotional side of things – rightfully so – but no one really talks about the practical things, or the trials and tribulations that go along with them. Things like all of a sudden none of the utility bills are in my name even though I was the one who would do our banking and see that they were paid every month. Or how to change the sparkplug in the lawn mower. Never did I think that my life as a single woman would involve that. Needless to say, if you need to know, I'm your gal.

My daughters and I continued to live in that house for 6 years after my husband left. We had always been a team, but those years brought us even closer. We all learned and grew together. I was able to teach them things as I was learning them myself. They were able to see, first hand, that we could do anything that we set our minds to.

Those years were filled with victorious days when we, as a team, would accomplish a "man job". I have a great respect for men who are handy-dandy. And let me tell you, it's sexy as Hell to me to watch a man do some "manly" shit. However, there is also great satisfaction when I could do one of those things myself. I loved showing my girls that we could do whatever we put our minds to. I'm a half-in/half-out feminist, I guess. I know that I can do all of that stuff on my own, but I also love the notion of a man doing it for his woman. I work hard to instill that into my daughters. Be smart and resourceful enough to be able to do what you need to on your own, but have the grace and humility to know when it's ok to let someone else do it for you. That's a woman's wisdom.

———

Ugh.
You know you're probably going to piss people off with that.
What if they don't get your humour?
Yes, I know you crack yourself up on the daily, but not everyone has as sophisticated a sense of humour as you.
See?
That was hilarious.
Do you think they got it?
Are they laughing?

———

3

I have always had a massive fear of appearing weak. Of being weak. Helpless. Incapable. There were so many times in those years when I felt exactly that. When I became what I felt was the worst thing anyone could be. It was in those moments that every single demon that followed me my whole life would rear its ugly head. It was those times when I hated him for giving up so easily. When I hated myself for starting that conversation that night. When I was disgusted at the weak, pathetic woman that I was in that moment.

For most people, having a partner means you don't have to feel those things. You each naturally pick up the slack or fill in the spaces that the other isn't strongest at. At least, that's how it was for us. Those times when I couldn't do whatever it was, I questioned if I'd made the right decision. If it was all worth it. I wondered if this was my punishment for me daring to believe that there was more out there for me. There were days that I spent in my bed, in tears, raging, screaming. Pleading with God to give me a sign that I had done the right thing.

I can't recall all of the signs that came, of course, but I do remember one thing that impacted me so intensely...

I was in my room. Sitting on my bed. I was crying – loud, ugly, raw tears. The kind that are accompanied by the sounds that we usually try to stifle. My (ex) husband had done something regarding financial support for me and the girls. That was his M.O. Money. He had a lot of it, and the girls and I had none. That was a power point that he often used. And it worked. Money equals power in our world and by those standards he had it all, and I had none. Feeling weak and powerless was/is my Achilles' heel, and he knew that. Normally I was able to keep my head clear and could fight back, but this time he made it under the radar.

My oldest daughter came to my room. She was 14 at the time. She was calm. She was hurting for me, I could see it in her face, but in that moment, she was the calm in that storm. She stood there, seeing me. Listening to me. I was sobbing, "It wasn't supposed to be like this! I'm a good person! I don't understand!"

Over and over, "It wasn't supposed to be like this...."

My daughter, with all of the compassion and wisdom of infinite lifetimes said to me, "Mom, just because it's not the way you thought it would be, doesn't mean it's not the way it's supposed to be."

Let that sink in.

That one statement from my child cleared all of the clouds from that moment for me. That, ladies and gentlemen, was the Divine at work.

That moment will stay with me forever. For so many reasons. But also, it showed me that these were the moments that were worth more than gold. These were the moments that made every single shitty thing worth it.

The emotional part of that time was brutal. It was exhausting. High highs and low lows. The worst part for me, I think, was the anger. Ugh, the anger was unlike any other. It was laced with feelings of unworthiness and injustice. With betrayal and rejection. It was fueled by a childhood of trauma and toxic dynamics. That is a powerful combination. I'm usually a pretty calm, albeit emotional, person. But there were moments when I literally just screamed with the pressure of it all.

I would spew hate and profanities into the Universe about my ex-husband. It would be so irrational, but also so fucking cleansing. You know? Because in those moments, my guard would be completely down. I would let out every single thing that had been building inside of me. I would unleash every dark thought about myself that I kept hidden away…every fear, every wound, every emotional burden that I had been carrying my whole life.

Of course, there were the times that I directed all of that at him, and I'm not proud of those times, but I am only human, after all. I own those times and apologized for *some* of them. (like I said, I'm only human)

There are many books available about how to navigate through the end of a marriage. There are courses and counsellors. Everyone who has gone through it has their own advice. For me, I kept remembering how it felt to go through my own parents' divorce. THAT, was my guide. My daughters were around the same age that I was, so I accessed those memories of mine and did my best to see that I behaved differently than my own parents did.

Even though I was a kid – I was 11 when my dad left – I was still old enough to be talked to about what was happening. But I wasn't. No one sat me down and told me that my dad wouldn't be living with us anymore. No one told me that it wasn't my fault, or that I'd be safe and loved. It was this giant fucking elephant in every room of my life and not one person ever thought beyond their own selves to talk to me about it.

Now here I was, a parent to two incredible daughters who loved their dad very much, and I could either recreate my history, and perpetuate that cycle, or I could rewrite it and break that cycle. I had the opportunity to be the parent that I needed when I was going through that. And that's what I did. I sat my girls down and told them what was happening. I reassured them at every opportunity that they were so very loved. I encouraged them to ask me whatever they needed or wanted to know and I promised them that I would always be truthful with them. Because I knew how it felt to be kept in the dark. To be afraid and sad and angry and hurt and have no one to tell me that it was all going to be ok. That I was loved. That I mattered.

In offering that to my own children, I was also offering that to my inner child. To my eleven-year-old self. That was the beginning of my healing. That was also the first cycle of toxicity that I vowed would end with me.

I think that in making that conscious decision, that was also the first time that it occurred to me that I could change the future. That history didn't have to repeat itself. That I was strong enough to face that demon and banish it for good. I think it was also my first realization that healing isn't always about releasing white doves into the sky to the singing of an angelic choir. It's about digging deep and getting your hands dirty. It's about unpacking all of that stuff that you have been carrying around for far too long. It's messy and gut-wrenching and horrible to relive it all, but it's also incredibly empowering to know that your children won't have to carry that burden that you passed along to them. And truly empowering to know that you're beginning to uncover a better version of yourself.

Let me be very clear, though, I do not have all of the answers. I teared up and felt a lot of resentment still as I typed that out about my own parents' divorce. It's something that I'm working to release for good. But I believe that bringing these things out into the light is the most powerful thing of all. Not to lay blame, but to bring them out of our own emotional shadows. To cast the light on them and see that they are real and valid and not something that we should have ever been burdened with.

This was the beginning of my return to self, although I didn't know it at the time.

———

Wow.
That was a lot.
I knew you were carrying that still, but I don't think I knew how heavy it was.
For what it's worth, I'm proud of you.
You've been so afraid of hurting people with this, but this is YOUR story.
This is YOUR truth. You're allowed to tell it.
Think of the people who could be encouraged to share theirs after reading this.

Well, I hope that at least someone is.
Ew.
You're getting a lot of crying fluids on the keyboard.
Don't use your shirt!!
Ugh. Ok, let's keep going.

———

Here's what you don't really consider — or at least I didn't — when you sit down to write a book about your own life and experiences.... there are other people involved in those things. I'll be honest, I struggled with writing this, very personal, stuff. I was afraid of upsetting my parents. It took me a long time to see that in doing that, I was minimizing my own feelings. Censoring my own story for the comfort of someone else. For everyone reading this (if you made it this far), your feelings matter. You are allowed to tell your story. Period.

PART TWO

4

Did you roll your eyes at the phrase *return to self*? It's ok if you did. What a hippie-dippy phrase, amiright? Aren't we always ourselves? Who the hell else would we be? Why do we need to return?

All valid questions, and as someone who has always spoken her mind and not been afraid to go against the norm, there were times in my own life when I would have asked those questions myself. But think about it, over the course of our lives we become many people – son/daughter, brother/sister, friend, girlfriend/boyfriend, employee, employer, spouse, parent. Those are just some of the roles that we take on in our life. Each one with a different name for us. Each one that requires the igniting or the shutting down of a part of us. When are we ever completely ourselves? Truly? For most, if not all, of our lives, we are playing the role of someone.

5

When one finds oneself single after many years of not, one needs to get familiar with not only herself, but with the world around her.

These next chapters will make you laugh, maybe make you cry, and likely make you blush. I've always known that I would include this stuff so it will be an adventure for me to navigate that process. There is a LOT to unpack here and so much that I know many will be able to relate to. Feel free to go grab a beverage before we begin.

I guess this is where I should put a disclaimer: I am not an angel. Nor am I a whore. There is a lot of territory between those two that I think isn't shown the respect or understanding that it deserves. Perspective is everything.

———

I can't believe you're actually going to tell this stuff.

You know that people you know are going to read it, right?

OMG what if this gets made into a movie someday?? Or a limited series, I know those are your favourite. It'll have to be on HBO for fuck's sake. It'll definitely need a rating above PG13.

Are you sure about this?

It's not too late to just skip over it.

Ok, it's your book. Knock yourself out.

———

(The truth is, I'm nervous to put most of what I have in this book. I talk tough, but I'm nauseatingly afraid of being judged and even more afraid of being rejected. If I had a dime for every time I've typed something, deleted it, then typed it again...well, let's just say I'd have a handful of dimes. But this might be my one chance to do this. I know that this is part of my destiny so who am I to not follow through? If I get judged, so be it. If I get rejected, so be it. It wouldn't be the first time for either of those things, and I'm sure it won't be the last.)

"*I think that who I truly am, is who I am when no one is looking. What I say when I think no one is listening.*

What I hear when I'm alone with my thoughts.

Maybe someday I'll have the courage to be that me always.
Better still, maybe someday I'll not care who is there to witness it or not."

-Jodi

6

Part of the agony that led to the end of my marriage was the lack of physical affection. I'm an affectionate woman. Physical touch is definitely one of my love languages. When that fades away, it leaves a really big space. I wasn't being dramatic when I said the thought of never being really, thoroughly kissed again was enough to make me feel like my soul was dying.

So, you can imagine that once I found myself single, I was practically desperate for that thrill of a first kiss again.

There were a few months when I practically leapt at any chance, I could get for a good old make out session. I didn't care about an emotional connection. I didn't care about sex. I just wanted that rush of a really great kiss. It was like a fix that I sought out. Having been deprived of that feeling for so many years, that quickly became all I could think about for a time.

Finding yourself single after years of not is akin to setting a victim of starvation loose in an all you can eat buffet. It's an orgy of self satisfaction and gluttony of what you've been starved for. The first couple of months were just a blur of release of some sort for me. But, after the initial thrill, I began to come back to reality. The binge of debauchery was over. It had done its job. I was initiated back into the world of the unwed.

Looking back on those months now it could appear to some that I wasn't really mourning the end of my marriage. I won't lie, it's not as though every day was filled with sadness or anger or epiphany. There were days that were just days. Days that I did rejoice in this new beginning for me. And days that the only release for the anger and sadness were just to go out, get drunk, and let loose. It's a strange transition period and one that I think most do go through. It's part liberation, part doubt, part anger, and part hope. It's messy and chaotic and unpredictable. There is no right or wrong way to move through that time. Mostly its just a blur that we try to survive.

On the other side of that initial time period is when I started to grasp that I had the chance at a new life for myself. I began to wonder what I wanted that to look like. Who did I want to be? Who did I want with me?

That meant entering the dating world. More specifically for me, the *online* dating world.

Online dating wasn't even a thing before I met my husband. And if we are being truly honest, dating wasn't either. I grew up in a very small town. People got together – usually courtesy of alcohol - and it was just decided that they were either a couple or they weren't. There was no "dating". We didn't even have a movie theatre. I had no idea how to date, and living in the same small community that I had grown up in, the only way I was going to meet someone new was to embark on a journey into the unknown...

7

By the time we hit our 40s, we should have a handle on how we view ourselves. We should have a feel for how we fit in, and move through, the world around us. If not brimming with confidence, we should at least be comfortable and well-versed in our attributes.

The online dating world will blow all of that to shit.

I'm not even kidding. It is a bloody battlefield. Allow me to set the stage... for me it looked like this - an online arena of 40-something men who, for the most part, have major baggage, unhealed trauma, something to prove, or are lost boys. My God. Nothing could have ever prepared me for it. As soon as my dating profile was live, I was bombarded by messages. Flattering at first, but quickly turned into a barrage of what-the-fuckery. Sexual invitations, attempts at conning money from me (can't get blood from a stone, sucker), creepy stalker-ish messages, foul tempered responses to rejection. I learned very quickly that I had to be very discerning and that I couldn't let everyone down easy.

It was an emotional rollercoaster and an exercise in human behaviour that both repulsed and fascinated me. The psychology and sociology geek in me was clapping its hands with glee to be witnessing such shocking behaviour, but the newly single woman in me was quickly losing hope.

I think it's also important to add that the men were not the only ones with baggage. I was carrying a full set of my own, although I didn't realize it at the time. Let's just say that when dating at this stage of the game, damn near everyone has their shit, and every single one of us is at a different place on our path to healing from some sort of rejection.

There's also the stigma attached to it. Stigma, I might add, that is solely from those whom have never engaged in online dating themselves. At first, I was so embarrassed. I didn't even upload a photo of myself. "What a loser", I'd think of myself. "Reduced to this."

You can imagine how well that worked.

Online dating is essentially catalog shopping for love. Without a photo, you have no idea what the hell you're even dealing with. I had to get over myself if I had any hope in Hell of moving forward with this.

So, I uploaded what I thought was a decent selfie of myself. Came up with a charming, witty, and insightful bio to add with it that I was sure would inspire any number of mind-blowing conversations with all the most desirable men out there, and posted my profile for all the world to see. At least that's what it felt like.

DING! DING! DING!

I started getting responses almost immediately! "Oh my God," I thought, "this is it! I'm going to have my pick! This is going to be amazing!!"

Let's talk about my first date, shall we?

To be honest, I can't even recall his name anymore. We messaged back and forth and spoke on the phone a few times. We seemed to have the same sense of humour. He was well spoken. His photos showed a handsome man.

We made plans to meet for lunch. That seemed safe to me. It was a set time frame that wasn't too long if I needed to get out of there, and wasn't too short to tell if we wanted to pursue date two.

I was SO nervous. Remember, I really hadn't dated at all in my life. Plus, I was armed with all of the horror stories of women being attacked and I had notified all of my "stand by in case I need you" friends.

I got my hair done. Make up went well. Good outfit.

I got to the restaurant and he was waiting for me. First of all, he had a very large port wine birthmark that covered half of his face. Honestly, I didn't care, but I quickly realized that none of his online photos showed that half of his face. Transparency would have been nice. But, like I said, it wasn't a deal breaker at all for me, just a surprise.

Now, I guess I should say here that I look quite young for my age. I always looked at it as quite a blessing and that I was aging well. Apparently for him it was weird. Every single time the waitress even walked past our table he would make some sort of comment that I was his niece. I shit you not. I laughed it off the first couple of times but then it just got to the point where I was like, dude, why are you being so weird?

We ate our lunch and the conversation was pleasant. He paid for the bill and we got up to walk out of the restaurant. I don't think I was expecting him to kiss me, but I was thinking he'd probably go in for a hug, which I was ok with. Well, neither of those things happened. He gave me like a bro punch on the arm and said "thanks. See ya" and practically sprinted away. I shit you not.

I thought the date was overall quite successful. Plus, the lead up to it was great – daily texts and phone conversations. I mean aside from the whole awkward niece thing, I thought it was worthy of a second one. I remember standing there, in front of the restaurant not knowing if I should laugh or yell what the fuck. I walked to my car and did both. Of course, there were a string of friends wanting to know how it went and the more I told it, the funnier it got. I said, more than once, "is this what is in store for me?" What a way to burst onto the dating scene. Baptism by fire, for sure. At least I got a lunch and a funny story out of it.

That was the beginning of what would be a very long and very illuminating path of dating and exploration for me. But this is all a very real part of life. Of next chapters. Of blooming. First of all, nowadays if you want to meet someone, you really have no choice but to eventually dip your foot into that online dating pool. I was in my 40s. I was not about to go to bars and meet someone. Desperate times, amiright?

So many people are embarrassed to admit that they have been on dating sites. I'm not. Like I said, how else am I going to meet someone? This at least increases the odds of doing so. And it has given me so much life experience that I'm so grateful for. Honestly, it's a part of my journey.

Needless to say, that first date didn't exactly give me much hope, but as I mentioned, it did give me some knowledge…

Note to self - Make sure that you can see their whole face from multiple angles in their photos!

As for the niece thing, I got nothin'. We didn't ever speak again after that so I have no idea what that was all about. Maybe he was in the midst of his own midlife crisis and coming to terms with his own aging. Honestly, who the hell knows. I take it as a compliment though.

I had many stops and starts. All of the men that I was conversing with lived at least an hour away from me in one of the two nearest cities. I quickly learned that for many, the world ends at their city limits. Good to know. Something else to add to my book of dating knowledge…

Many value proximity over connection!

That was a continual bone of contention for me. I would have what would feel like a great connection with someone, only to have it abruptly terminated when they learned that I lived an hour away. Nevermind the fact that most of them spent longer than that in their daily commute. (insert eyeroll here)

There would be those who just wanted someone to talk to, and I understood those ones. They liked having someone to tell about their day or to unpack that baggage to. I was a source for unloading for many. For the most part, I was grateful to be that for them, but it did get incredibly draining for me.

Sprinkled like fairy dust amongst all of that were the incessant hook up propositions. The unsolicited dick pics (yes, that is an actual thing). I could lie right here and say that I was repulsed by every single attempt made to get me into the sack, but I wasn't. I had spent years with a man who was rarely affectionate with me. With whom I didn't feel sexy or desired. I was a roommate, not a lover. To have men finally see me as a woman. To want me. To desire me, even if it was just in a physical, carnal way, felt good. To a degree it was even flattering. That might surprise some and make them clutch their pearls, but it's true. I am a woman.

W-O-M-A-N. I like to turn some heads and be the star in a few fantasies. Lord knows it had been a very long time since I had felt even close to being able to do that. That's not to give permission to, or excuse, the inappropriateness of a man just openly speaking to a woman that way, and it definitely doesn't excuse or even allow the unsolicited photos or attentions that cross numerous boundaries, but there were a few consensual conversations that I engaged in that I am definitely not sorry for. New experiences abound!

It was months before I agreed to go on another date. I have no idea who it was with. Clearly it was unimpactful for both of us. It was shortly after that that I decided that I would go on every date I was asked on for the next three months. I needed practice dating. I had no idea what it entailed, if I'm being totally honest. I was nervous and shy and wanted to be better at it. If I wanted to up the calibre of men I was meeting, I'd have to be a better date myself.

So, for the next three months I went on every date that I was asked out on. I was ONLY dating. Not looking for a relationship. This was some serious practical training. I think I went on over 20 dates in that time. All during the day (safety first). It was either coffee, or lunch or ice cream. All very casual and easy. Sometimes they would ask me, sometimes I would ask them. Whomever did the asking paid. Let me tell you, I got really good at the "first meet". I met some great men and some total duds. I learned so much about myself and about others. It was a great experience and I recommend it to anyone.

I had no expectations. It was all to get me out there and to learn and be better, and I would like to think it did the same for those men too. This was a part of me that I had never known before or even had the chance to cultivate. I was pushing my comfort zone, and that was definitely impacting – in a positive way – the other parts of my life. I was gaining a level of confidence that I really didn't anticipate. Let's remember that I was over 40. I grew up in an environment that implied all of my best years were now behind me. I also grew up in a very small community, in a small corner of the world. That led me to believe that I would either be alone the rest of my life, or would have to settle for someone that didn't light me up, if I wanted to avoid the dreaded being alone.

Fortunately, I have always been the one to march to the beat of my own drum. I didn't hesitate to look outside of my perimeter, in fact, there really was no doubt that that would be my course of action.

But I digress…

The whole dating thing was a massive growth experience for me. I began to learn things about myself that I would need to use discernment with. Let me preface this by saying that I have always been that person that strangers talk to, no matter where I go. I'm friendly and open and that is the energy that I give off. Which is a wonderful trait to have…unless you're in dating bootcamp with mostly wounded and needy men who have suddenly found themselves single with "no warning" (seriously…is there no eyeroll emoji for books yet?) My natural approachability and warmth would quite often be mistaken for attraction. Ooff. Having to kindly reject was also something that I became fluent in. And, much to my surprise, there were many times when I had to completely abandon my kindness and straight up tell someone to fuck off, thankyouverymuch.

I learned how very naïve I was, but also how to totally trust my intuition − even when I was lonely enough to almost believe whatever bullshit was being served. Growing up in a small community, everybody knows everybody so there are very few secrets or dark personality traits or even deceit in the mix. If you did it, someone always knew about it. That offered a level of security that I took for granted once I started dating in the big world. Also, the internet didn't exist when I was a single woman before my marriage. So, I also very quickly learned that not everyone was as up front as I was online. Not every photo was of the person that I would be messaging. Not every word of a dating profile was truth. Not even every word of private messages were!

My sharp intuition would help me to weed out the fakes and the scammers – of which there were many. Those who are quick to prey on the kind and often lonely hearts of many online. This was a major wake up and grow up call for me. The proverbial "We're not in Kansas anymore" realization.

It's amazing though how much you can truly learn about yourself in this situation. Not that I recommend leaving your current – happy – relationship just to learn all about yourself via the online adult dating scene. But it was an opportunity that I'd have never gotten had my marriage stayed in tact. God. That's such an absurd sentence. An absurd sentiment.

"Thank you, Universe, for leading me to the end of my marriage so that I could enter the ridiculous world of dating over 40! I've learned ever so much about myself!" *where's the sarcasm font on this keyboard? *

It wasn't all bad. I had some great times. I met some fantastic men. Had a few epic make-out sessions with zero strings attached. I even managed to find love....

Well, I guess we are in too deep to quit now. Are you sure you still want to go ahead with these next parts? That means you have to be all vulnerable and shit. You know those nightmares that you have when you're suddenly naked in public? Yeah. That's what it could be like. Just sayin'.

"*I hope that I never stop falling in love.*
Regardless of the heartbreak or vows to
never do it again.
I hope I do.
Over and over until I find the one that
sticks.
Because that means that I still believe."

-Jodi

8

I love love. I always have. I have a binder full of odes and essays devoted to the subject of love, all written by me starting way back in my teens. I still haven't had the full experience that I dreamed about, wrote about, but I'm hopeful that it will happen.

I met my husband on a blind date. I knew within an hour of meeting him that I would marry him, but I also heard very clearly in my mind that he would not be the love of my life. Those are the words that I heard in my head* as we sat across the café table from one another, drinking coffee and chatting. As mentioned before, I did love him. I've had the experience of loving many men. But so far, none have been the L-O-V-E that I've searched my whole life for.

———

this might be a good time to let everyone know that you're a psychic. Otherwise, they could be inclined to think you're off your rocker.

———

Looking back over all of the love I've declared in my life, it's interesting. I have a perspective now that allows me to really look at what all of that was. I've heard it said that we can only meet someone where we ourselves are at and never before have I realized that, or seen it, with the clarity that I do now.

I'll be honest, I hoped that there would be love for me after my marriage, but there was a part of me that was like, "What if that was it? My one shot? What if that was as good as it gets?" That was a depressing thought, to say the least. But at the same time, I never had the opportunity to be fully me in that relationship, in any relationship, so there just had to be more. Right?

Becoming more myself, more of who I am at my very core, meant that I had to be willing to love, because love has always been the ultimate goal for me. I was still learning about myself though, so it was a gamble, but isn't it always?

I've been fortunate enough to find love on this path – a few times. The firsts were messy, intense, scary, exhilarating, painful. They made me realize the wounds that we all carry with us into each new relationship. I was always one to believe that love could fix anything. Maybe it can. Maybe what we think is love isn't really love because it *didn't* mend anything at all.

When I *was* in it, and when I *am* in it, I am IN IT, it feels real and whole and magical.

… until it doesn't.

At the time, in the moment when the magical haze begins to fade, it's so easy to lay blame. It seems so clear, so evident. And I suppose in some ways it is. But the more I began to know myself, the more I realized what I brought to that table as well.

You see, it's not just the men that I was encountering who had the baggage. I had quite a lovely matching set of my own. At the time though, I thought I was self-aware enough to be free of it all. HA! Good one, Jodi. What I recognize now, is that each of these men that I shared feelings, or other bodily fluids, with were sent to me for my own healing. For my own growth. Gradually, I began to see a progression in each fling or the relationships that I entered in to. I could see how each built upon the one before – from both sides. They became beautiful stepping stones along my path.

The first actual relationship that I entered into after my marriage was over was with a man that I met online. He lived some distance away from me, as was/is the norm for me seeing as I live quite close to where I grew up.

We began chatting online and I quickly realized that I had a rapport with this guy that I hadn't ever had with anyone. Same sense of humour, which is a huge thing for me.

We chatted quite often and it was always fun and lighthearted. We decided it was time to meet, but there was a catch…

It turned out that he wasn't who he said he was. Well, his personality was exactly who he really was, but his photo, name, etc. was not. This definitely triggered my trust issues and I felt completely betrayed and to be honest, quite stupid. We couldn't deny our personality match though so we decided to be just friends.

Of course, that didn't last long. I think it was inevitable that we would end up being more, and that's exactly what happened. This was a relationship that was so completely different in a million different ways from my marriage. It wasn't judgemental. It was very honest (even after our deceptive beginning), and I don't know that I ever laughed so much with a man, ever. Lord, did we laugh.

It was also so easily affectionate. I've always been an affectionate woman but had to severely tone down that part of me in my marriage because my attempts at affection were often unwelcome. Not with this one. I remember my oldest daughter telling me one day that she thought it was so weird, "but in a good way, Mom", to see me being so affectionate with someone. When I asked her why, she told me because she didn't ever see me and her father acting that way so she didn't know that such thing was possible/acceptable. That really struck me with how much we don't realize our children are absorbing from us. As parents, we model "acceptable" behaviour in so many ways to our children. It made me so sad to think that my daughters were growing up thinking that it was "normal" to not have playful affection in a partner. It also made me so very relieved to know that they wouldn't have to think that anymore.

We were together just around a year, I think. It became increasingly more obvious that we both had some baggage and a lack of self-love that we needed to address. We also had a major breakdown in our physical relationship, despite our affections. This was something that was especially triggering for me and was something I also dealt with regarding my ex-husband. It's funny how the things we need to address and heal the most will be placed right in front of us. This was something that I knew I needed to work through, but wouldn't understand the full weight/breadth of until years later.

So, we parted ways. It was very sad for us both because we were each other's "first after". We were the relationship training wheels that we both needed to reintroduce us back into the wild.

When I look back on this to see how this brought me closer to me, I would have to say that it did so in many ways. It reminded me how very important laughter and affection is to me in a relationship. Laughing is incredible medicine. It releases endorphins, raises our energetic vibration, and is a perfect reminder that life isn't − and shouldn't be − all serious. I find that as adults we often forget that. It also felt so good to laugh with someone whom I really *liked*, and who liked me back. Big, belly laughs with someone you love is really fucking sexy. It is an excellent reminder of all the things you love about that person. It had been a long time since I had felt that. It reminded me how high on the list of importance it was for me − as it should be!

It also gave me a judgement check. This man had a colourful past, to say the least and normally I would hear about someone like that and immediately write them off in my mind. I would judge them before I even knew anything more about them. This time I didn't. To be honest, by the time I found out about his past, I was already feeling love for him so I wasn't about to run. Whatever the case may be, it forced me to pause and listen rather than make a snap judgement and shut it all down. We all make mistakes. We all have moments in our lives when our choices are less than stellar. His consequences just happened to be a little more severe than the average 20-something. It was good for me to have that perspective from someone.

As I mentioned before, this also made me acutely aware of the importance that I have always placed on the physical part of any relationship. I equated physical want and connection to love, and although I know this is a huge part of a healthy relationship, it can get distorted and manipulated when it's rooted in limiting beliefs and pain. The emotional baggage that he carried into this relationship greatly impacted our physical relationship and that forced me to come face to face with that big ole wound inside of me. I didn't exactly sit down with it, but I began to acknowledge it's existence.

Ultimately what this relationship gave me was hope. That I could love and be loved. That it was possible to find someone who laughed with me and enjoyed my company. It showed me what I could build upon.

9

The next time I felt love, I was more aware of what I brought into that space – good and bad. I held on to the perspective that I had gained so far on my path. I felt like I was ready to try my hand at this relationship thing again.

This one was everything that the previous was plus more. Laughter, affection, friendship, plus this one had the physical component that my wounded self needed. Woooo!! Off to the races!

I thought this one was my one. I truly did. And he was, for a short time. It turned out that his wounds and baggage was enough to put us collectively over the allowable limit.

We all have baggage. Especially when we are in our 40s and have a marriage and multiple relationships in our past. Add to that our limiting beliefs that we have carried and narrated our lives with since our childhood, accumulated trauma, and real-world problems. It's amazing that anyone can fall in love with anyone else, to be honest. It's a downright miracle.

This one moved in with me and my daughters even. It was much shorter-lived than I had hoped, but it was just the way things needed to be. Like I said, at this stage of life, it's very rarely just about two people in a relationship. There are many others involved as well. It's not always about what we, as a couple, want, it becomes what is best for the whole. I loved and respected that very much.

It was during this relationship that I really began to lean into my writing. I had started my website which was then just a blog, I submitted, and had published, a piece for a popular website online. I was testing out the waters of who I really was – who I am – for the first time in my life. I felt safe enough and confident enough to do that, and he was very supportive. What a unique thing for me to experience! Someone who was proud of me and supported something that was just for me.

We had some big adventures. He had a pastime that was as fun as it was unique and I loved being exposed to it. It took us to picturesque places in the gorgeous Canadian Rockies that I'd have otherwise never seen. It meant road trips with singing to 80s music and long conversations. I loved it and sharing this part of his life with him.

This was also the catalyst for another big realization for me… I had a habit of diving into and fully supporting whatever it was that the men in my life were into. Like, DEEP diving. I can hear some of you say, well that's not a bad thing! It's great to have shared interests! Yes! It absolutely is wonderful to have shared interests with the person you love. *Shared* interests. Shared. It was in this relationship that I realized that I always made a point of learning about and supporting the interests of my partners, but it was never reciprocated.

I remember after my ex-husband moved out, one of the first things that I did was cancel all of the channels on our tv that I never liked. Oh, I watched them. All the damn time. I knew shit about shit that I really didn't even care about. But my husband did. So, I would watch poker and hunting and golf and God knows what else because that's what he was into. It sounds so silly, but with him gone, my daughters and I could finally watch what WE wanted to. Something that I had honestly not even given any thought to before. What a simple thing to provide such a realization.

Now please don't think that I am trying to make myself some sort of self-sacrificing wife/girlfriend of the year by admitting this. I'm not at all. What I'm saying is that I didn't realize the extent of the lengths I went to in the hopes to make myself more…. I don't even know…. loveable? Wanted? I know now that it was from a place of wounding than a genuine interest. In the case of the man in this relationship above, it was definitely tinged with "look how much better I am in your life than anyone else has been". Even though I did genuinely enjoy it, my motives − subconsciously or not − weren't always pure. I realize that now.

Towards the beginning of the end of this relationship we were driving back from somewhere (most of our relationship was in a vehicle, I swear), and we were talking about how I didn't feel seen or supported in the relationship. I remember saying that all we did was centered around his life and his interests. He said to me, "But you're not even *into* anything!" I still remember that moment. That feeling. Not into anything?? I was into a million things, but we were both so consumed with his interests, that he didn't even bother to recognize that I had many of my own. That was a defining moment for me, and for us. Once again, I was so easily minimizing my own self in order to − or in hopes of − be more lovable to someone. Evidently that didn't end when I cancelled those stupid tv channels.

As I said, that was at the beginning of the end of the road for us. Pun intended. I feel like there was a deep love for one another there, but there was clearly also deep wounding. That's not the most ideal foundation to build anything lasting upon.

So, there I was. Alone again. More realizations about myself. More clarity about what I brought to the proverbial table, and what I still lacked. More insight and perspective about what I need from the person that

I share my heart and space with. More aware of me. More aware of them. I was in a place where I could start to look back and see the stepping stones that had appeared on my path after my marriage ended. There were more than before, but as I was not at any discernable destination, I knew there had to be many more ahead.

10

As of the writing of this, there has been one more love.

So far, it's been the one that has gifted me with the most growth, the most learning. It's incredibly sacred to me and I honestly struggled with whether or not I wanted to include it here. But it has been pivotal in my life thus far and I truly can't speak about becoming more myself without at the very least, mentioning it.

It's interesting to note that I was never ever disenchanted with the hope or idea of love. If anything, I think I became more determined to find it. Once I could see the building blocks that each man who came into my life brought with him, no matter how brief or how long the interaction, I just knew that it all had to be leading somewhere. To something. Hopefully to someone.

I wasn't looking for this one. I am almost a fanatic about observing human behaviour and in my quest for just that, this one came into my life. It was a mutual appreciation for observing and dissecting choices, behaviour, needs and wants.

It was vague and sporadic conversation. Random check-ins with zero expectation on either side. An easy friendship. Was I physically attracted to him? Oh my word, yes. My pulse quickened at the sight of him. Corny, but true. Was he physically attracted to me? Yes. Something that amazed me. But as I said, neither of us was looking for anything other than someone to share musings and observations with.

It's funny when you don't have any expectations of something, how that thing can be surprising in the best ways. We lived at a distance from one another. I was working a job that I loved and had started my own business on the side. I was finding my groove in my life with my daughters and it was good. I was also in some sort of sexual awakening that was incredibly empowering. I was discovering parts of me that I didn't even know existed. I liked what I found. A lot.

It felt like *this* was where that path with the stepping stones was leading me. Every day I was becoming more and more Me. I was learning so much about what I was capable of as a woman, as a mom.

When you put that energy out into the world, the Universe will reflect it back to you. I was falling in love with me. With this version of myself that finally felt good and...*right*...for the first time in many, many years. And the Universe answered in kind.

This one showed me my toxic behaviours that I had leaned on for decades and gently asked, "why?". Then waited patiently while I figured it out. That alone was astounding to me. First of all, to be called out on my bullshit... The emotional blackmail that I didn't realize I always employed when things didn't go my way. The lashing out when my abandonment wounds were triggered. The pushing away when my fear became too great. And then to not have them used against me. To not be punished for them. To be gently, compassionately, and lovingly held accountable for them. This is what it meant to hold space for someone. A phrase that I had heard and read often but had literally no idea what it truly entailed. This was no ordinary love.

Remember in post-marriage relationship #2, I realized that I had never had "shared" interests in any of my relationships? This love turned that on its head too. Common interests aplenty, but also a genuine and sincere curiosity and interest in my life and what lights me up. Support of my endeavours. Something that I had never, ever experienced before. This created a safe space for me to speak up about not only my interests, but my thoughts, opinions, knowledge. It made me realize that I deserve a seat at the table, not just to set a place for someone else. Self worth. Something that I struggled with my whole life.

This love taught me patience. It helped me to define what grace means to me. It instilled the importance of allowing. These are all huge things that, as a very spiritual woman, are incredibly important for me to not only understand, but to at least experience, if not embody.

This love was a journey into the heart of me – literally and figuratively. I had unbecome who I was for so very long, and transformed into who I was meant to be...or at least had given me a substantial start.

This was the love that felt like the culmination of all the others that came before it. Just as each one had felt. In the moment, in that space of love that I was in with each one before, I was at the apex of that path, the trailhead of where those stepping stones had led me. Each time I felt, at least at some point, that the path didn't go any further than there. Each time, I was wrong. I don't know if this one really was where all of those stones led to, or if there is more beyond this. What I do know is that I had gotten closer to who I feel I truly am and meant to be than ever before.

———

I came in here to add that this love also came to an end. It really did a number on my heart. I came closer than I ever have to not believing anymore in my happily ever after.

The things that I learned from this — about me, about people, about life — are incredible.

Although my hope has dimmed a little in intensity after this one, it is still clinging to life. Maybe if I get the courage to get back onto those stepping stones, they will still lead me to where I've been searching...

PART THREE

11

It can't all be love and romance, can it? I mean, I wish it could be, but there are many other facets to this heart of mine − and of yours, I'm sure.

This path to becoming me is a wind-y one, for sure. Every time I thought I had reached a part upon which I could coast for a bit, the Universe stepped in with other plans. It makes me think of that part in the movie Shrek where Shrek and Donkey are talking about how Shrek is more than just an ogre. He has layers, like an onion. I'm beginning to think that I'm an onion too...or at least this journey to myself is.

Let's talk about my physical body. I've always had a love/hate relationship with it. I've certainly always taken it for granted. I can remember dieting in high school when I didn't need to, but because I was built differently than the girls around me, thought I had to.

I can remember trying to hide my feminine-ness under baggy pants and shirts. An hourglass figure is not something that most young adults appreciated back in the 80's and 90's.

I also remember having potent sensuality before I even knew, or appreciated, what it really was. This was a strange thing to possess when I was continuously trying to accept my body. Thinking I was "too fat" and being embarrassed of my size and shape. Men would always respond to me differently than my friends and it would always take me off guard.

There was a period of my life when I would not honour my body at all. I smoked, drank, slept with anyone who turned my head and made me laugh. I cycled through binge eating and starving myself. I was always active though, so my body was very physically strong. Now I would call it resilient.

When my marriage ended, as most of us do, I began to focus on my physical body again. I decided to take up yoga. A few more rounds of this diet or that. I've always had this type of reverse body dysmorphia. I would see myself as slimmer in the mirror than I actually was in reality. It would be a total mind fuck when I would see a photo of myself and that image would not line up at all with what I saw in the mirror every day. I would struggle with any sort of consistent confidence in my physical appearance.

One day I was getting my lady bits sugared (it's an ancient form of hair removal – look it up), and having a conversation with my sugarist. We got talking about body confidence and how every single one of us deserve to feel amazing in our bodies. Sexy. Fierce. Like a Goddess. At the time I was returning to the ever-punishing world of online dating and my body confidence was taking a shit kicking. When you're a curvy or plus-sized woman, you're either considered fat, or fetishized by most men. It's exhausting.

Back to this convo between me and the woman who was ripping my pubic hair out by its root... She was showing me these gorgeous photos that a girl she knew had taken and posted of herself online. Now, I grew up with actual cameras that had film in them. Our selfies consisted of turning the camera to face us, hoping that we were in the frame, and then waiting for the film to come back from being developed. The world of cell-phones definitely made that whole process easier, but I was still very run-of-the-mill when it came to my self-portraits.

But seeing what this other girl was doing was amazing to me. At first, I thought, oh I can't do that, that's so embarrassing. But then I thought, well, I'm alone. It's not like there's anyone else in the room to see me flirtatiously smile at the camera or toss my hair in that (hopefully) sexy way.

So, I went home and started taking selfies. Different angles. Different smiles. Different lighting. I began to see myself on that little screen as I saw myself in my own mind's eye. It was liberating and empowering. I quickly updated my online dating profiles with these fabulous new photos. It worked! The messages started flooding in! Again, most were trash, but one or two caught my eye.

There was one in particular. He was a handsome man. A total silver fox. Well written profile – he could actually spell and knew how to use punctuation. Nice photos. Ticked a lot of my boxes. We began chatting. He was enamoured with me. Told me every time we spoke how beautiful I was and that he couldn't believe that 'someone like me' was attracted to him. I'm not even kidding. I had never been spoken to that way. I haven't again to this day. It was amazing. It felt so good.

We began making plans to get together. We were both excited for it. My confidence was at an all-time high. I took a photo of myself in a new maxi dress that I had on and sent it to him.

After a pregnant pause, he messaged me saying that he didn't realize that I was the size that I am and that he was no longer attracted to me.

I wish I could say that I made that up. Read it again if you need to. I know that I read his message multiple times trying to make it make sense.

Mere seconds before, this man adored everything about me from my eyes and my smile to my fantastic sense of humour and confidence. But the size of my body rendered all of that moot.

What. The. Actual. Fuck.

And to be clear, I was not huge. I was what they now call mid-size. So much for that body confidence that had been growing, right?

I'm tough, but not bulletproof. That hurt. The rejection. UGH. The rejection. All based upon the size of my physical body. That one thing suddenly negated all of the other amazing things about me that he couldn't stop fawning over?

Of course, I know now that he is a shallow piece of trash and the Universe totally did me a solid on avoiding that one, but at the time, it hurt like a mother fucker. I allowed myself a few days to wallow in my self pity but then I got pissed off. Who the hell was that guy, anyway? What the hell did he know? I'll show him and his kind what they are missing.

It was time to up my selfie game....

———

Jodi. Listen to me. Are you suuuurreee that you want to share this next stuff? Like…sure, sure?? Once it's out there, it's out there. No take-backsies…

———

…I'm sure.

Actually, I'm not, I'm feeling a bit nauseous about it, but I'm not ashamed of it, it's just that fear of judgement and rejection. Go into this next part with an open mind, ok?

———

12

So, what was going to be the difference between these new selfies and the ones before?

SPICE, BABY!

This time I was pissed. I had an axe to grind. I had something that I wanted to prove − to myself, and to all dicks like that guy. I created an anonymous social media account, came up with what I thought was a catchy name, and got busy. This time I needed to look at myself through totally different eyes. I had to try to see myself as sexy. Flirty. Goddess.

You would think that would be easy, right? Not exactly. As women, we are taught to hide that side of ourselves. That it's shameful. I had to break through a lot of mental walls to even take that first selfie.

To be clear, I was not naked, nor was my whole face even showing. It was a flirty, sexy, tease of a pic. Lips and cleavage. Posted anonymously. As scary as it was, it was also incredibly liberating. Empowering. I couldn't stop looking at that pic. I couldn't believe that was me. I freaking loved it.

I spent the next few days when I was home alone, coming up with different outfits and ideas for my new persona. Taking pics. Posting them anonymously. No one was following me. I was just posting them for my own sake. It was so much fun.

Eventually a few people found my account and began following me. Then a few more. Then more still. Before I knew it, I had over 5000 people following my account. Women and men. Wanting to see my photos. Complimenting them. Calling me sexy. Classy. Cheering me on. Wanting me to pay attention to them. Offering me money. It was crazy! Intoxicating. It changed the way I walked, and moved and saw myself. It gave me the confidence to not only embrace who I was, for the first time, but to celebrate me.

You need to remember that at this time I was 45 years old. Divorced. Mom to two teenaged daughters. I was curvy and unapologetic about it, for the first time in my entire life. I had men and women cheering me for embracing my body and all it's societal imperfections. That is incredible. It still blows me away when I think back on it. I was receiving from strangers, what I never once received from anyone else in my life, especially myself. Instead of considering myself the fat one of the group, I now knew I was the powerful one. The sexy one. The get-the fuck-out-of-my-way one.

What's even more interesting to me, this feeling, this confidence, spilled over into the rest of my life. I carried myself differently. I stood up straighter. Engaged differently. I felt so comfortable in my own skin for the first time. It was incredible. All because of some judgemental dickhead with a fat phobia.

I kept on with my secret account. Eventually I got bold enough to show my face. I began to let my personality come through in my photos and posts. Always, I was accepted. Complimented. Applauded. It was amazing to me. Even in my own personal circle my friends weren't that supportive or encouraging.

Author's note: If your friends aren't your biggest cheerleaders, get new friends!

Now as a mom of two amazing young women, I was always conscious of what I was doing and how they would perceive it. I made a personal rule to never post anything that I would be ashamed of them seeing. My oldest, being the intuitive and psychic that she is, knew that something was up with me. She didn't need to be psychic to see the changes in my confidence. When she asked me what was going on and what I was up to, I told her. Then I showed her. She was surprised, but not shocked. She applauded me as well. She appreciated the trail I was blazing and the chains that I was breaking by embracing my own sensuality.

Soon, I had messages from people asking if I had any of my photos for sale.

"What?! Ew! No! That's weird!", was my immediate response.

Wasn't it? I mean, who the hell would *pay* for a sexy/flirty photo of me???

As it turns out, many.

I shit you not. I had people actually paying me money for my photos! Always tasteful (which I was always complimented on), yet totally steamy. I ended up having quite the side gig by selling my selfies. It still boggles my mind. My daughters and I laugh at how that Christmas was funded in large part by my "secret photos".

You might be wondering why I am including all of this in this book. To be honest, I debated adding it. But it was a huge part of my life for a good year. It helped me to break through some shame and guilt around my sexuality. It gave me the immense gift of seeing that at 45, I was still desired. It also gave me a new perspective on sex work, because let's face it, even though I was not putting it "all" out there, it was always intended to seduce, tease, entice. There's no shame in that. In fact, I think every single woman over 40 should learn to see themselves as a sexy, sensual, being. Hell, I'll even go so far as to say that I think every woman over 40 should have their own "secret account" where they can let out and explore that part of them.

That was a part of me that I had kept hidden all of my life. Women are expected to be and do and don't and then we are expected to be openly judged for all of it, all of the time, at every stage of our lives. Fuck that. If you can create a space where you are free to be you, and are embraced for it, do it. You deserve to be all that you are.

————

It was a great year of sharing that part of myself. It was eye-opening in so many ways. Did you all know that there are multiple sub-cultures in your everyday social media platforms? I met some incredible, fascinating people that I never would have met otherwise (a Dom with actual sex-slaves and who trains women who are interested in learning more about that lifestyle winning the prize for the most jaw-dropping of them! For real. We met in a Starbies and he was the most accountant-looking, non-descript, unassuming man ever. It was a fantastic conversation and I'm sure my eyes were the size of dinner plates the entire time! Haha! Don't worry, I wasn't there to sign up for his training, it was just to satisfy my morbid curiosity.).

That account is still active today although I very rarely post on it. It takes a lot of effort, to be honest. You have to be in a certain headspace and I'm not always there. It's fun to drop in on it once in a while and post a pic when I'm feeling feisty. It's also good to be able to look back on and see that part of me. Especially on the days when I have forgotten what it feels like.

If you take anything away from this chapter, I hope that it is the inspiration, permission, or even the curiosity, to take a sexy selfie. To see yourself through those eyes. If you're male or female, it doesn't matter. We all have that inside of us, and we all deserve to see ourselves as desirable.

———

Ok. That wasn't so bad. Listen, I don't expect everyone to read this and be like, "Ok I totally get it!". But this was a major part of my journey and one that I don't think I would have been able to embrace at any other time in my life. In a world where women over a certain age are often disregarded, it felt super powerful to show that it's not always the case. Do with that what you will. It's ok, I won't judge you for it.

PART FOUR

"When our bodies speak to us, they always start with a whisper. If we don't pay attention, those whispers will soon become screams."

~Jodi

Ok loves. This next part could be activating for those of you who have surgical trauma in your past. I still get those feelings now, 4 years later. It is an important part to tell and a huge chapter of my late blooming.

Deep breath.

Here we go...

13

We are now entering the "shit's about to get real" part of my story. Not that the rest hasn't been real, but this next part is really-real. Pretty much the realest.

My new-found confidence had meanwhile helped me to sell my home. The same home that I had lived in with my ex-husband and that I had raised my daughters in. I was moving them out of our small community and to a larger place where they would have a better life. It was a stressful and emotional process as I sold it privately, and having never done it before, I was learning as I went. I'm not sure that, had this happened a couple of years prior, that I would have had the confidence to do all of that on my own. See what a boost in self confidence can do?

I digress…

I was also going through more legal battles with my ex-husband at this time because he had decided to go against our divorce order and then play dumb about it. That's a whole other ball of wax. I would like to say here, however, that financial abuse is very real and very much abuse. Something that my children and I were subject to for the entirety of my marriage, and beyond.

Needless to say, it was a very stressful time for me. I began to feel run-down. I felt physically weak. This pissed me off because if you'll recall from the first chapter of this book, I hate not being able to physically do things. I chalked it up to stress. It made sense when I thought about it; my divorce had finally gone through after 6 long years, I was then back in legal battles with my ex due to his breaking of our divorce settlement, I sold my home of 13 years privately. That is a lot of stress.

I got my daughters and I moved, the legal stuff settled, and still wasn't feeling a whole lot better. The fatigue was real. Still, I *had* just gone through a lot over the past year so I knew I was physically, mentally, and emotionally exhausted. I surprised my girls with a trip to Disneyland for my youngest's birthday. Just pulling my suitcase through the airport was a chore for me. "Boy, am I ever out of shape", I said to the girls.

If you've ever been to Disneyland, you know that it is basically bootcamp. You walk from sun up until beyond sundown. It's day after day and mile after mile. If you're a Disney lover like we are, it's totally worth it, but it's still exhausting.

This was my second time here and I didn't remember being so tired whilst walking all day. I didn't recall needing to stop and catch my breath, or having to walk so slowly. Just chalk it up to the stress of the past year, and keep going.

Those were the whispers.

On one of our Southern California vacation days, we went to Universal Studios Hollywood. So much fun. Sunshine, no crowds. It was perfect. My oldest and I decided to go through The Walking Dead attraction, as I was a big fan of the show. Honestly, I don't remember much of it. Between screaming at the zombies approaching me, and laughing with the group of ladies behind me, it was a blur. My heart was pounding in my chest.

We exited out, my heart still pounding, and all of a sudden, I felt like I was going to pass out. I had never felt that feeling before, but it's strange, you just instinctively know what it is. I was extremely lightheaded. I scared my poor girls who rushed to get a staff member to come help me. After I sat down and drank some water, all was well in a few minutes. We chalked it up to too much excitement and the zombies being a little too realistic.

The rest of the trip passed without incident and we returned home and I vowed to get in better shape so I wouldn't be the one to slow us down on our next vacation.

All was well. I joined the gym, started working towards getting back in shape. I was still exhausted, but began to think it was chronic fatigue. I was healthy and strong, after all. Overweight, yes, but still strong.

Our Disney trip and that incident were in September. At the end of November, I had a second one. Followed closely by a third. This time I was on a romantic getaway with the last person that I spoke of a couple of chapters ago. We were walking down a particularly steep hill to get back to our rental car as we were headed to the airport. This one hit me the same as the first did. Heart pounding from exertion, then dizziness, then feeling like I was going to pass out. Again, as with the first, it passed in a couple of minutes. It returned, however, as we were walking quickly to our departure gate at the airport. I checked my Apple watch this time to see what my blood pressure and heart rate were at. Blood pressure was pretty ok, heart rate was low to normal. Again, it passed. By this time, I was more embarrassed than anything else. I was so mortified that I was *this* out of shape and had caused this man, whom I loved so very much, to worry.

. . .

The whispers were getting louder.

Over the next four months these "episodes", as I began to refer to them, would happen whenever I over exerted or stressed out my body. I was concerned, of course, but I had no chest pain whatsoever, they always passed within a few minutes, and I was just tired, and stressed, remember?

April 3, 2019, I started my day like any other day, except I had a hair appointment booked. I loved my hair appointment days. My hair has always been my crown and that was one of very few splurges I had on myself. I came home from my appointment. Let my dog, Sophie, out into the backyard to peepoops since she'd been inside for the last three hours. While she was outside, I came into my room to get changed, but first, I wanted to take a picture of my hair, because I loved it so much and fresh hair is the best. I took a pic and wanted to open my blinds to let some sun in so the colours in my hair could be seen better. As I opened the blinds, I looked into the back yard and noticed that our back gate had come open. We had just moved from the country to the city so I was terrified that something would happen to Sophie and I ran outside.

Sophie is my best girl, second only to my daughters so I was just sick with fear and worry. I ran down the deck steps and down the alley, calling her name the whole time. As I got to the street, I saw her and as soon as she spotted me, she ran back to the yard, thank God. I ran back behind her, tears streaming down my face and my heart racing with the thoughts of what could have happened to her. I made it halfway up the deck stairs when I suddenly fell down onto my hands and knees. Another "episode", but this one I knew was different from the others.

I don't know how long I was like that for. A few minutes. The whole time I was praying so hard for God to let this one pass just like the others. After I'm not sure how long, I managed to get up and get Sophie and I into the house. I went into my room to try to calm myself down and continue praying and willing this episode to go away. It had already lasted way longer than any of the others. Although there was still no pain, this one felt different. More significant. This one scared the shit out of me.

I was home alone. I finally was feeling well enough to call the health help line. I spoke to a nurse and told her what had happened. I told her of the stressful time I'd had the year before. Because I'd been born with a heart murmur, she advised me to go to the emergency room to get checked out, just in case.

Now, you might be wondering why I didn't mention this heart thing before now. Well, it's because it had never been an issue for me. It was found when I was 9 years old and although I had routine check-ups with a cardiologist, and had to take preventative antibiotics whenever I went to the dentist, I had never been affected by it in my life. And remember, I didn't have any pain or tightness in my chest at all when these "episodes" would occur. So to me, it was irrelevant.

Something else about me that is worth noting – I'm not a big fan of going to the doctor. I had an amazing doctor for most of my adult life, but he took a leave from his practice to pursue some medical teaching in Africa. He was the only one I trusted and he got me. He knew that I didn't go to the doctor just for fun, if I was ever in his office, it was for something big. He also, quite literally, saved my life when I was battling post partum depression. He left some very large, and special, shoes that I was quite certain no other doctor would ever come close to filling.

Both of the above things made me hesitant to go to the hospital on this day. That, and I was afraid. I called my oldest, who was on her way home from work by then, and she raced home and convinced me to go to Emergency to get checked out.

The whispers had become screams.

14

I'll spare you all of the details, as it could be triggering for some – truth be told, it still is for me some days – but some are important to this story and of my growth.

I was admitted to the ICU after a barrage of tests in emergency. My heart was screaming for help. Looking back, of course I could see that it had been for months. I was on strict orders to move as little as possible and was scheduled for an angiogram in the closest major city. I was very afraid, but put on the brave face for my daughters, and thankfully, my sense of humour stayed firmly in place. The patient board in my ICU room had me listed as "Your Majesty", at my request, and I was quite certain that the EMTs that came to transport me via ambulance were in fact, a stripper-gram sent by a friend. Sadly, I was wrong on that one. It was still good for a giggle, and they were definitely easy on the eyes.

My angiogram was something of a full-circle moment for me. I had had one when I was 9. It is when they feed a catheter through the main artery in the groin up to the heart. They then inject dye and take pictures of it to see if and where there are any blockages in the heart. I remembered the procedure from almost 40 years ago. I carried that with me into this procedure. I couldn't stop crying. Maybe it was the combination of reliving a wounded part of my past, and being able to drop the brave mask that I had been wearing so I wouldn't scare my babies. One of my nurses, as well as the doctor who did my recent angiogram had worked with my childhood cardiologist and spoke so highly of him. What a small world, we all agreed. They were all so incredibly kind and did an amazing job of comforting me throughout the procedure.

I was wheeled into recovery where I had to remain motionless on my back for an hour (harder than you would think), and pretty soon I was again surrounded by doctors and nurses who had gathered to talk to me about what they had found. My aortic valve was so diseased, it was barely functioning. I would be admitted to the hospital immediately and not leave until I had open heart surgery to replace the damaged heart valve. The doctor who performed the angiogram said to me, "So, I heard that your dog got out and after you chased her, you collapsed and that's what finally got you to go to the hospital. Is this true?"

I said yes.

He said, "Well, your dog just saved your life."

Cue the waterworks again. Or did they even stop? Who the hell knows, honestly.

———

Ok a big aside here....my dog, Sophie, is my best friend and soul mate. The only souls I love more than her are my daughters. Of course, it was she who "saved" me.

———

Another doctor comes in. So kind. So patient with my blubbering. Explains to me about my heart valve and why I need a new one. Asks if I have any questions. I had a million of them, but didn't ask any of them. I was so afraid. More afraid than ever before in my life. I had never broken a bone. I had never had surgery of any kind. Now they were telling me that I was going to need open heart surgery in the next few days. My head was spinning. I actually think that a part of me was in denial. It was so strange.

This was a Friday. All of this had begun two days ago, on Wednesday. What the hell was even happening?? Two days ago I was at my hair dresser's, laughing and talking and taking pictures of my fresh hair. Now I was literally coming face to face with my own mortality. What the actual fuck.

One of my best friends from childhood stopped by to see me briefly that same day. We kept it light. Short and sweet. But I could see in her eyes that she was freaked out too. This not only brought me face to face with my own mortality, but hers too. We didn't speak of it, but I'll never forget the unspoken worry in her eyes. We weren't even 50. We sure as hell had never acted a day over 25. This was weird and uncomfortable.

But soon my girls were with me and it was back to my brave face. I would be damned if I would have them be afraid or believe anything less than the very best outcome for all of this.

Did I ever tell you that I had considered suicide once? Not now, not because of this. It was nearly 17 years prior. I had been struggling with depression for a couple of years and I finally reached a point that I felt it would be better for everyone around me if I unburdened them of the constant worry that was me. The only thing that saved me that day was my babies. I couldn't bear the thought of them being alone with their mommy's lifeless body so I made one last plea for help. That was the one that worked. I fought for myself because of my babies that day, and every day since. I wasn't about to stop fighting now. But holy shit I was scared.

The next couple of days were filled with tests and scans and bloodwork and decisions. Conversations with my cardiac surgeon, the anesthesiologist, the physical therapist. All preparing me for what was to come. Reassuring me. Sitting with me as I cried and cried. Listening to my fears and doing their best to assuage them.

I was in a room that held 6 people. Men and women. Ranging in age from 20 to 80. I didn't know any of their names, yet I was witness to some of their most vulnerable moments. I didn't chat with any of them. Not to be rude, but because we were all in our own world in there. Simultaneously trapped with our thoughts and desperately trying to escape them.

I quietly observed though. Something I've done all of my life. The combination of my intuitive abilities and my love of studying human behaviour was perfectly suited for just this.

There was the farmer's wife across from me. Her husband would be there first one there every morning with her coffee in hand, and he'd be the last one who left every night. I could tell that she was his rock and this temporary role reversal was throwing him for a loop. I'd guess they'd been high school sweethearts – each other's first everything. She ran the household while he did the work outside. He likely wasn't one to express his affections or appreciation of her, but they had a solid foundation and routine that kept them strong. Her being in the hospital with her own heart issues clearly brought him face to face with a possibility that had never once crossed his mind – life without her. It was sweet to hear them whisper and giggle when they thought the rest of us were sleeping.

Beside her was the grumpy Gus. I'd say mid 60's, looked to be in good shape, this was definitely not on his 5-year plan. He had a very particular way that he liked his little area to be. Curtains closed just so, bed tray in the optimal position, along with the things upon it. The bathroom door opened to the exact degree he determined. He would get very agitated if any of those things were moved, and he would curse and mutter under his breath while he readjusted it all back to their rightful place.

At first I thought, 'What a dick. None of us chose to be here, he could at least get some perspective.'

But then I looked closer. I paid attention. He was every bit as afraid as the rest of us. This was a man who had control over every aspect of his life and now he was facing something that he had ZERO control over. The only way he could deal with his current situation was to control what he could – the curtain, the bed tray, the door. Once I understood that, I didn't see him as grumpy at all, but human.

Beside me was an adorable older man from, I'd guess, Eastern Europe somewhere. I'd say he was in about his late 70's or early 80's. Quiet. Kind. His wife would come in and they would hold hands and giggle and tease one another in a language I didn't understand. I'm guessing it was a combination of years spent together and their native tongue. He was due to be released and he and his wife waited and waited, never getting impatient, so gracious. When the doctor came and told him that he would need to spend one more night just to be safe, he didn't complain. He said, "I have another day to give. I trust your judgement." He was just the sweetest, most gentle soul in the room.

Finally, there was Kasha. The only one who's name I knew. She was a 22-year-old young woman – a girl, really. She had lost her arm to cancer and was currently on the waiting list for a heart transplant. She had the most infectious laugh and had friends visiting her every day. To listen to her talk with them about the latest happenings with their friend group or how she couldn't wait to get home to play her PlayStation, you'd never know the massive weight that was hanging over her every second of the day. Whenever she caught my eye, she had a big smile ready to go, and she was always saying hi to my girls when they were there.

One day her doctor came in and was talking to her about her transplant. He was quietly explaining to her that if they didn't find a donor heart for her in the next 5 years then she wouldn't survive. This usually positive and vibrant young girl spent the rest of the day curled up in her bed, crying softly.

I cried with her. For her. As afraid as I was for my own surgery, it was considered involved but routine for the surgeons there. It gave me a perspective and a bit of courage to understand how truly blessed I was to be in my position. I think of her often and hope that she is happy, healthy, and has received a new heart.

15

I won't go into all of the details of my surgery, because that's not the point of this. The point is to share the perspectives that I was given as a result of all of this. How allllll of this contributed to the person that I am now, today, as I write this, and as you read it.

I didn't sleep much the night before my surgery, if at all. I was in a space of avoidance and fear laced with a bit of positive thinking for show. I was terrified, to tell the truth. The nurse came in at 5 to wake me up and take my vital signs. My girls were already there with me. I don't imagine they slept either.

We are a tight team, us three. Even though none of us was saying the 'what ifs', I knew we were all thinking them. I was in a horrible space of feeling the need to tell them everything that I might need to share with them over the next 50 years, in case the worst happened, and staying brave and positive for them with a 'see you later'. I landed on telling them both how much I loved them over and over and over.

This is where I pause and cry it out for a bit, remembering that.

Being faced with the very real possibility of never seeing the two true loves of my life again was the absolute worst thing I've ever experienced and I wouldn't wish it on anyone.

I cried until I went under for my surgery.

16

I don't remember a lot after I woke up from my surgery, but I do remember being so relieved that I did. I'm not going to lie and say that I knew it would all be great and I'd come through the surgery with flying colours – I did my very best to hold on to that thought, but there's always that fear…

Something else that I haven't spoken a lot about in this book so far is my spiritual self. I'm a psychic and medium. That's a massive part of who I am. You might be asking, 'well, then didn't you KNOW you were going to come through surgery?' On some level, I'm sure I did know, but the truth is, psychics aren't very good at looking at their own lives and potential outcomes. That's the caveat to having these abilities, I suppose. I did, however, know that my mom's best friend, and one of my most favourite people, who had passed around 7 months earlier, was with me throughout my surgery.

This was confirmed in a mediumship reading I received a few months later when she described my very crooked scar perfectly.

It's funny, because of my otherworldly abilities, I was half expecting to have some big experiences and revelations whilst being under anesthesia. I don't know what, but *something*. In hindsight, I guess I'm glad that I wasn't privy to all that was happening.

I cried a lot after my surgery. They were different tears than the ones that I shed before. These ones were borne of a heart that had been cracked wide open. Literally and figuratively. Everything had happened so fast. It was less than a week between sitting in my hair dresser's chair, laughing and joking, and undergoing emergency open heart surgery to receive a mechanical heart valve. My whole world had been turned inside out. I'm a planner. A bit of a control freak. Even though this was part of the grander plan, it was a surprise to me. Those of you who don't deal well with the unexpected will know what I'm saying.

This also gave me insight into the people in my life whom deserved to be there – and who didn't. This unexpected event in my life was gifting me with perspectives that I maybe wouldn't otherwise have. I suppose it was a new standard with which to hold myself and others up to. I had a new compassion for myself and others, that empowered me. It's hard to describe. On the one hand, I was more perceptive in the battles others were facing, but on the other, I knew it could not always be an excuse for being a shitty friend or family member.

This would be the beginning of the end of some very big relationships in my life.

Ok you even got me crying there. I know that I give you a hard time – it's my job – but I'm proud of you for how you handled all of that. I didn't know you had it in you. Ok, maybe I did, but I'll never let you know that.

I cried my eyes out writing these chapters. I cry every time I read them. Reliving it all. It was the first time I put some things into words. Even though it was the scariest thing I've faced in my life thus far, I'm grateful for so much. To be alive, for one, and the gift of perspective that I wouldn't have received otherwise.

PART FIVE

"I honour myself first, and in doing so, am able to honour the relationships that I have with others"

~Received during meditation by Jodi

17

As with any major event in our lives, it can be very telling as to who is there for the long run, and who's journey with us has come to an end. I've learned to be grateful for these times, although that doesn't make the process any easier or hurt any less.

I've also come to realize that not everyone goes through these releasing periods. On my sad days, when I'm feeling lonely, I envy those people.

Divorce is a great divider. I had already gone through that. I had lost a great number of people in my life whom I thought would be with me till the end.

Major personal events, such as illness, injury, or surgery are also great shedders of light on boundaries and relationships. This had never occurred to me until I had gone through my own. Looking back on it all now, I know that some people were perhaps reliving their own traumatic experiences that were triggered by my surgery. I cannot fault them for putting as much space as possible between me and themselves. They were protecting their own mental health. I get it.

But there were others, many, who just went radio silent with no explanation. As sad and in some cases, pissed off, as that made me, I was able to eventually get to a place of gratitude for that truth. Far be it from me to judge anyone who doesn't have it in them to pretend.

I never realized how the path to myself would result in the shrinking of my circle. I always had a circle of friends. As with everyone, it ebbed and flowed and morphed over the course of my life, with a few core members staying.

I just assumed that my core group would remain my core group for the rest of our days. It never occurred to me that even that core would be susceptible to the passage of time.

Listen, I changed a lot over the years. I feel that the biggest changes occurred after my marriage ended. I had the freedom and opportunity to explore who I was, who I wanted to be. It surprised me and made me a little sad even to realize that maybe what held us all together was not something that I had in me anymore. My core had been my core for most of my life. In many ways we defined one another. Who was I if I wasn't part of that group anymore?

I don't feel like enough is said about the loss of friendships as we move through life. They are often longer relationships than the romantic ones. We are encouraged to go through therapy and the process of grieving when a romantic relationship ends, but not a friendship or 6. It's strange.

I am absolutely not trying to make myself out to be a victim here. Truth be told, it was my decision to walk away from most of the friendships that I did. It was not an easy decision, but one that I felt I had to do in order to pursue myself. To be who I so desperately needed and wanted to be. I had outgrown that familiar circle. The one that had seen me through all of the major events of my life. The one that filled my memories and photo albums. I still miss them all the time, but much like trying to squeeze into a pair of jeans that you've been saving for "someday", we just don't fit anymore.

You never know what it is in life that will make you evaluate who has access to you or your energy. For most, it is a big life event. For others, it's a nudge or whisper that just says, "not anymore". It happens though. To everyone. And I think that's ok. I think its as much a part of life as everything else, but it's just not as addressed as much.

For me, it was everything, I think. My marriage ending, moving, surgery. Those are all big things that made me shift my perspective on a lot. On where I put my energy. On the conversations that I wanted to have. I could feel the gravity of it all pulling me away from the life and friends – and family – that once surrounded me.

I never in a million years thought that I'd find myself so completely isolated from those who were my lifeline for most, if not all, of my life. But I guess I had been given a perspective that encouraged me to say "no more" to some of the things that I had allowed to impact me, my energy, and my emotions for so long. I won't get into all of it here – Lord knows that it could be a book all on its own. I will just say that in pursuing the life and path that honoured myself, I had to place distance between me and those who didn't. Friends, family, acquaintances. I'm sure from the outsider's point of view it seemed that it was a simple thing for me to do. Let me put it here, in black and white, and say that it was, in fact, quite the opposite. The road to truly loving and honouring yourself is not an easy one at all, but no one seems to talk about the fallout.

———

This was a strange part for me to write. I very much love and miss my friends and my estranged family members and even though this is MY story, I am mindful of their feelings. A therapist would have a field day with that, wouldn't they? Cue my people pleasing tendencies and need for acceptance!

The truth is, it's painful. It's divisive. And to be honest, I'm sure some people are going to read this book just to see if I slander them. Haters gonna hate, amIright?

Yet, it IS a part of my journey. My endings of these valuable relationships have shaped who I am and how I move through life. It needed to be in here, vague however it may be.

I want you to know that if you have experienced these types of endings, I see you. I feel your pain, and also, I applaud your deep devotion to your peace.

PART SIX

18

Here's the thing.

While all of the above was happening, I was also going through the biggest spiritual awakening of my life so far. I have always been spiritual as opposed to religious. I have always been fascinated by mysticism and magick and other beings from worlds yet to be discovered by us. I always believed in fairies and aliens and Bigfoot. I knew God was real and angels were everywhere and when we died, that wasn't the end of us. But it wasn't always at the forefront of my life. First of all, it wasn't as socially accepted or as mainstream as it is now.

Do you remember at the very beginning of this book I was talking about being on the blind date with the man that would end up being my husband? As we sat across from each other, drinking coffee and talking, I heard a voice as clear as day in my mind that said, "You are going to marry this man, but he won't be the love of your life". I remember it very vividly. This didn't freak me out. It didn't startle me or alarm me. It just was. I've been experiencing things like that, and others, my whole life. So I was already very much believing and spiritual.

My ex-husband was very black and white. He was raised Catholic so believed in God because he was taught to, but I don't know that he ever really, truly believed, you know? Anyways, he was of the mind that he needed proof of things before he would believe in them. Because of that, I kept my spiritual experiences and beliefs quiet for the duration of our marriage. Once in a while I would bring something up, or experiment with my own abilities, but for the most part, they were met with silence or doubt, so it was easier for me to just keep them quiet.

He suffers with migraines and one night he could feel one coming on and I asked him where it was located in his head. As we laid in bed, I energetically travelled inside of his head to where his headache was starting and I visualized relaxing and untangling the blood vessels there that were causing his headache. I didn't say a word while I was doing this. After a few minutes of me focusing my energy on this he told me that his headache was going away. I'm pretty sure I fell asleep with a smile on my face that night.

All of this to say that my spirituality was still very much a part of ME, but not always a visible part of my life.

Until my marriage ended.

Suddenly, I was free to fully lean in to my spirituality. To my gifts and practices. So that's what I did. I began to meditate and I was given my first deck of oracle cards (thanks Mom). I began to research and read and learn and talk about things freely and openly. My daughters are also very spiritual and open minded so we had many, many years of interesting conversations and experiments.

The house that we lived in was very active spiritually. My ex-husband would even see our shadowy roommates and commented on them more than once. We would see shadow figures walking through our kitchen all the time, and we were always feeling a cat rubbing against our legs when there wasn't one there. More than once I tripped over a cat that I swore was at my feet, just to look down and see nothing there.

The spiritual path isn't all love and light and rainbows. In fact, I totally hate the phrase, "love and light" and it gives me the heebie-jeebies. Far too many use it as a passive aggressive catch-all for their ignorant and intolerant bullshit…. sorry…I got a little derailed there.

The spiritual path to oneself is a messy and complicated one. It's isolating and emotional. At times it's far more darkness than light. It holds a mirror up to you and forces you to look at yourself and your relationships under a microscope. Imagine that all happening while I was learning to date, while I was falling in (and out of) love, while navigating friendships and family dynamics, and while facing my own mortality. It's a fuck of a lot. It's also a chicken and egg situation. Was I going through all of those things because I was leaning into my spiritual self and abilities? Or were those things happening because I was exploring who I am at my core? My guess is that it is a little of both. All of it was playing a massive part in the me that I have become, that I am becoming.

19

In case you haven't already surmised, I'm not your typical spiritual person. Well, not the internet's or social media's idea(l) of what a spiritual person is. I don't fit the aesthetic of the slim, vegan, matcha-sipping, sun-kissed yogini. I don't walk around clutching mala beads and smelling of incense. Nor am I a fit for the modern, girl-bossing spiritual bad-ass that has also made recent spiritual appearances.

I'm a 50-something overweight, divorced mom of two amazing humans who plays Mario Kart every night before bed. I love documentaries about cults and bingeable limited series streaming tv shows. I swear like a trucker (although I'm trying to cut back on that), eat too much chocolate and love science. I don't blindly follow or believe anyone or anything. But I have faith. Deep faith. Big faith. And hope. Bushels of it.

I'm also a multipotentialite. Look it up. Watch the TED Talk on it. It changed my life. Oh, and I've recently discovered that I have ADHD and am on the neurodivergent spectrum. That wasn't a surprise to me or my children. Haha!

Being spiritual is both and adjective and a verb to me. It is who I am, but also what I do. In my own way. On my own terms. I think that my age and my life's experiences enhance my spirituality. They definitely allow me to be able to relate to a large number of people on a level that I wouldn't be able to had my life been different.

I guess that's why I wanted to write this book. First of all, who the hell am I to think this shit show is book worthy?? Second of all, why did I feel the need to share it with the world?

Here's the thing…as much as I am an open book, I'm also not. I've spent so much of my life feeling like I was alone and that I was the only person going through the shit I was going through. Oh I know, everybody has their shit, but nobody was talking about it with me. Nobody's shit was similar to mine. I was already the odd one in my life, and add to that, my shit seemed to be different than the standard shit that those around me were experiencing.

It would have meant a lot to know that I wasn't alone.

Back in 2015 I submitted a piece that I wrote to an online publication. It got accepted. My first public exposure for my writing. It was a personal piece about my marriage ending and how life kept on (sound familiar?). The number of comments, messages and emails that I received after publishing that from people telling me that they finally felt seen and that they had felt the same things that I did, was a game changer for me. Men, women, all thanking me for sharing and making them feel less alone. For as long as I can remember, that has been my quest, to share what I've gone through in the hopes of letting someone else know that they aren't alone.

So that's why I'm writing this. That's the basis of my spirituality and work. Maybe even my purpose.

I'm a professional psychic now. I connect with Spirit on behalf of people who feel drawn to work with me. Isn't that amazing? Maybe this was always the plan, but I don't know that I would have the confidence to do this every day had it not been for the things I've done over the last 10 years. The crazy stuff. The scary stuff. The beautiful stuff.

This path was always leading to me. Not back to me, I'm nowhere near who I used to be, nor would I want to be. This path has been leading me to who I am becoming. I don't know what the next 50 or so years (God willing) have in store for me. But if I'm feeling more like myself now, at this point of my life, it stands to reason that I'll continue to get closer and closer to who I truly am. Discovering, learning things the hard way, exploring what I didn't have the space or courage to before.

I hope that you do too. I hope that this crazy decade of my life has held space for you to embrace your own journey to yourself. To do crazy things. To do what you feel called to do. To discover who you are and to become more of that person.

I haven't brought about world peace or cured any diseases. I don't have the answers to life's big questions. I can't even, in all honesty, tell you how to become more of yourself. I can tell my story. I can share my experiences. I can tell you that who you think you are, or have been, isn't the end of it. That you have discoveries and adventures coming that, if you let them, will teach you amazing things about yourself and the world you live in. That the best isn't over, it's probably not even happened yet.

I can tell you that like me, you can also be a late bloomer.

EPILOGUE

Wow. You did it. Finally. How many freaking years and do-overs

did this take? Now to see if anyone reads it.

———

Here it is. The story(ies) that have been rattling around my brain for the last however many years.

This isn't a how-to. You might not come away from reading this with any new skill or knowledge. But maybe you'll have a sense of feeling seen. Maybe you'll feel inspired to peel back those onion layers to get to the heart of who you are. Or maybe you'll just think, "what the fuck did I just read?".

Regardless, I hope this gives you the permission to bloom at whatever stage of life that you're at.

ACKNOWLEDGMENTS

I was told to think of this as my Oscar speech. To that end, I'd like to thank the Academy.

Just teasing.

There are some people that I would like to thank.

My ex-husband and the father of my amazing children. We haven't seen eye-to-eye for many years, but thank you for my most precious gifts.

To the others whom I have loved, and those whom didn't make the cut, thank you. You each brought something to my life that was needed at the time.

To my Spirit Guides – Lord knows you don't have it easy with me. Thank you for being my team.

To Sean, thank you for believing in me right from the start. Thank you for your patience. Thank you for your guidance. Thank you for cheering me on. I'm proud to consider you my friend.

Finally, to my daughters. Thank you for being you. Thank you for the gentle, and sometimes not-so-gentle reminders to write. Thank you for being my biggest fans. I couldn't have made this journey, let alone written this book, without you.

ABOUT THE AUTHOR

Jodi is a mom, business owner, professional psychic and lover of writing. She rarely passes up the opportunity for a well-timed "that's what she said", loves coffee, swears like a sailor, and wears her heart on her sleeve.

Jodi currently lives in Southern Alberta with her beloved pets and oldest daughter. This is her first book, but not her last.

Manufactured by Amazon.ca
Acheson, AB